All About
Steve Wozniak

Paul Freiberger & Michael Swaine

BLUE RIVER PRESS
Indianapolis, Indiana

All About Steve Wozniak

Published by Blue River Press
Indianapolis, Indiana
www.brpressbooks.com

Distributed by Cardinal Publishers Group
A Tom Doherty Company, Inc.
www.cardinalpub.com

ISBN: 978-1-68157-097-6

Author: Paul Freiberger, Michael Swaine
Editor: Dani McCormick
Interior Illustrator: Amber Calderon
Book Design: Dave Reed
Cover Artist: Jennifer Mujezinovic
Cover Design: David Miles

Printed in the United States of America

23 22 21 20 19 18 17   1 2 3 4 5 6 7

Contents

All About
Steve Wozniak

Introduction

Computers are in your life all the time, quietly doing all kinds of jobs. Your phone is really a computer. So is the family car. Computers are part of everything from refrigerators to TVs.

Steve Wozniak had computers figured out as a fourth-grader. He's the same kid who said that the logic that computers use "became the heart of my existence, there in the fifth grade."

Steve was a nerdy kid, to be sure, but he may not have ended up being the kind of person you'd expect him to be. He went on to do some great things with his life, things you'll recognize when we catch up with him years later.

He didn't spend his time as some kind of electronics hermit. He put on music festivals, he was on *Dancing with the Stars*, and after he became a multi-millionaire, he decided to spend a lot of his time teaching kids about computers.

Steve was a huge part of making Apple the company it is today. His work influenced computer design and development in remarkable ways and touches our lives in places far beyond Apple. His story is a lot more interesting than the one you'd expect to tell about the life of an engineer.

Steve Wozniak is not the man people think of first when the story of Apple is told. They usually think of Steve Jobs. However, our Steve has his own compelling story. His name is Stephan Gary Wozniak, and while he may not be as famous as Steve Jobs, his story is just as important.

Chapter 1
Early Impressions

He was born Stephan—not Stephen—Gary Wozniak in 1950. His story starts with a spelling error. It's an odd glitch in the life of someone whose work would be all about making complex things work with elegance and precision.

Margaret Wozniak meant to name her son Stephen with an "e," but somehow it got spelled with an "a" on his birth certificate, making him "Stephan." He chose to ignore the "official" spelling and go with what his mom had wanted. It wouldn't be the last time Woz ignored what officials expected and did what he wanted.

"Woz." That's what the other kids in the neighborhood called him. It's what his co-workers would call him later in life. Woz is the name he's always gone by and that he's made famous. It was never the kind of name that fit well with formal institutions like schools, colleges, and corporations, but things like that never seemed to bother Woz.

Despite the glitch of his misspelled name, his early life seemed almost engineered for someone who would spend his life with computers and technology.

Margaret Wozniak pushed her children to succeed and encouraged them to find their passion

Woz grew up in the Santa Clara Valley of California in a suburb that was surrounded on three sides by fruit orchards. In many ways, it was a classic 1950s setting: a group of modest single-family homes where the dads went to work, the moms mostly stayed at home, and the kids played in the neighborhood.

This was the beginning of the tech center of Silicon Valley, and the dads were mostly engineers working in the local electronics and engineering companies like Lockheed and Sylvania. The kids mostly played with electronics.

Woz's dad, Frank Wozniak, was no exception. Someone told Woz that his dad had been a football hero in college. It didn't click for Woz. To him, Dad was an engineer, first, last, and always. As for what he did, that was a real mystery. He worked at Lockheed, Woz knew. But dad wasn't allowed to talk about his job. It was all top-secret missile work, and talking about those projects was strictly forbidden.

Woz's dad worked for Lockheed,
which made planes and missiles

Talking about electronics in general, however, was a different story, and here Woz truly lucked out.

Having an engineer for a father meant that there were always tools, wires, and electronic components like resistors available in the Wozniak household. A kid interested in how things worked had something concrete to focus his curiosity on.

And Woz's dad had a gift for teaching. He was happy to help his son learn about the field he knew well. He was good at customizing his explanations so that they made sense to Woz, even when he was young.

But his dad didn't dumb things down for Woz. He just took it step-by-step.

One day, Woz found some resistors on the kitchen table and asked what they were. His dad didn't answer him directly. Instead, he started from scratch with an explanation that built up from atoms and electrons and went on for weeks.

Woz wasn't bored. He really wanted to understand, and his dad's step-by-step teaching was just what he needed for real understanding.

That step-by-step approach to learning a subject, where you start at the beginning and gradually build on that, is the method that Woz stuck to throughout his life. As a result, Woz always knew that his solutions went to the heart of the problems he was trying to solve. He knew that they were fundamentally sound.

As a child, Woz played with his siblings and mom and enjoyed getting new gadgets for Christmas

There was something else Woz was getting from these lessons in engineering. Woz's dad was proud to be an engineer. He loved what he did. And Woz picked up that passion. He began to feel that life as an engineer was the most interesting and enjoyable thing imaginable.

He also saw that it was useful, and that made an impression on him, too. Engineers built things that other people needed. So an engineer could do a lot of good in the world. From the beginning, Woz was convinced that all this learning had to be worthwhile for everyone.

All of those things came together in Woz's first real electronics project when he was just six years old. It was impressive for his age.

The project started with a crystal radio kit his dad gave him, along with a challenge. Woz's task was simple. He had to scrape a bit of the gunk off a penny, attach a wire to it, and touch that wire to some earphones.

He could hear voices coming out of the air! He'd found a radio station. He didn't know or care what station. But he knew that "something big had happened."

He told kids at school about it, and they had no idea what he was talking about. For Woz, it was exhilarating. He knew he had done something that most people assumed was beyond a little kid's ability.

Woz was always fascinated by the technology and circuits his dad had around the house, like his HAM radio

Woz was proud of his accomplishment, but there was something else happening too. His tiny project left him thinking that this was just the start. If he could do this, what else was out there that he could master?

As Woz went through grade school, that feeling about the future became more and more real. This was to be the first of many, many projects to come.

Chapter 2
School Projects

Some of Woz's projects were school activities, but his love for building things wasn't confined to that space.

A lot of it happened in his neighborhood, helped along by a group of friends he called the Electronics Kids. Most of those kids were, like Woz, the children of engineers. They also had access to garages and workshops full of wires, tools, and parts, all of which they were perfectly willing to put to use.

These were the days before computers and cell phones let us talk to each other whenever and wherever we liked. Their big project was an intercom system that connected a bunch of their houses. Woz was responsible for the design. It involved wire strung all over the neighborhood, terminating in switches, microphones, buzzers, and lights in each Electronic Kid's bedroom.

Secrecy was critical, as this was a kids-only, parents-prohibited project, and Woz designed it so that loud buzzers could be turned off late at night. Instead, lights alerted kids of incoming communications.

Woz strung cables between houses in his neighborhood so he and his friends could talk to each other

At first, the Electronics Kids used it for the sheer pleasure of seeing that it worked. Later, they used it to make arrangements for sneaking out of the house at night. Woz appreciated this practical purpose. However, the real thrill for Woz was that he'd built something, and that it actually worked. That would have been enough to justify the work he'd put into the project.

At the same time, he was a regular entrant into, and frequent winner of, school science fairs.

His first entry, and win, was a homemade flashlight, essentially a bulb, a battery, and some wires mounted on a piece of wood. Was he proud of that win? Yes. As Woz himself admits, winning has always mattered to him. But there was a side to that win that made it almost a disappointment.

"I felt inside that it really wasn't that impressive." He vowed to do better the next time.

In fourth grade, he took two carbon rods and a lightbulb and ran an electrical current through them. Then he dipped the rods into an assortment of different liquids. Each liquid would result in a different level of brightness for the bulb. By checking that brightness, you could tell how well the liquid conducted electricity. That's not just an important topic for science fairs. It's a topic that matters in the real world, relevant to everything from batteries to hydroelectric machines.

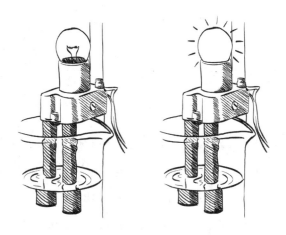

Woz tested conductivity of liquids
as one of his science fair projects

Woz didn't stop there. His next project, in fifth grade, was an interactive one, the kind of thing you might find in a museum of science today. It was an electrified layout of all the elements in the periodic table of the elements, complete with switches that allowed you to select an element and light up its electrons in their specific orbits. It won another first prize. Again, though, the prize wasn't as important to Woz as the feeling of accomplishment and the learning the project involved.

Two things made Woz's sixth grade project special. First of all, it looked something like a computer. It was a machine that could play tic-tac-toe, a game that works according to a strict and simple logic, the kind of thing that computers do so well.

The tic-tac-toe machine introduced Woz to the world of digital logic, the world that's governed by 0s and 1s in which something is either on or off, with no in-between. That on-or-off world is still the world of digital machines today.

The other thing that made it special was a little different. For once, Woz's project didn't win. In fact, it was worse than that. It literally blew up. The night before the competition, the machine's transistors started smoking, and there was no way to trace and correct the problem in time for the judging.

Ending up with a bunch of charred circuits was a disappointment for Woz, but he wasn't crushed. He was proud of what he'd built and what he'd learned, with or without smoking transistors. Losing took nothing away from that sense of accomplishment.

He wasn't proud of his seventh grade project, but in the eighth grade, Woz followed that first unsuccessful computer-like project with something closer to an actual computer. It was a machine that could add and subtract. Unlike the tic-tac-toe machine, this one had a practical purpose: the same purpose, among many others, that we expect computers to have today. Woz's "Adder/Subtractor," as he called it, had a real-world use.

Given that this was back in the day before computers were routine in our lives, this was a pretty special project. Strangely enough, though, Woz didn't walk out with the blue ribbon. And it wasn't because another competitor showed up with a working nuclear reactor.

Picture this: Eighth-grade Woz shows up at the contest the night before the judging is supposed to happen. He carefully sets up his machine. A group of adults stop by, and they ask him to tell them something about what he's built. Woz declines. He figures he'll wait until tomorrow, when he can explain it to the judges, rather than go through the whole thing more than once.

Perhaps you already suspect something that somehow never occurred to Woz. That's right: these grown-ups wandering the exhibits weren't random sight-seers. They were the judges. This had been his chance to show off what he'd built.

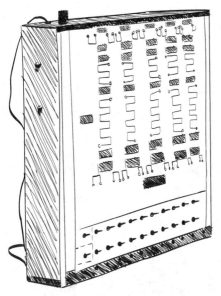

Woz's Adder/Subtractor was a sort of home-made
calculator and took a lot of work

And in the end, tomorrow was too late. He'd missed his chance. His entry never really got its moment in the spotlight.

That's Woz all over: a little shy, not too good at playing the angles, happy to assume that he had it all under control. As was to happen more than once over the years, Woz had his scientific bases more than covered. It was the people side of things that gave him trouble.

Even though he didn't win, Woz looks back on the project as a success, partly because he'd built a useful personal computer in its simplest form, but mainly because it taught him the virtue of patience.

The Adder/Subtractor used over 500 electronic parts, including transistors, diodes, and resistors. Putting it together and making it work was a long haul.

"I learned not to worry so much about the outcome," he says, "but to try to do it perfectly."

This was the mindset of the best digital engineers, the designers of computers. That is what Woz was becoming.

Woz didn't get the chance to show off his project,
but he was proud of his work nonetheless

Chapter 3
Pranks and Tricks

It may sound as if Woz's early years were nothing more than a series of electronics projects. Your image of Woz may be of a kid hunkered over a circuit board, soldering iron in hand, getting the next machine ready and doing little else. But that's not quite right. Those projects were definitely milestones, and they meant a lot to Woz. But he wasn't hiding in the garage all those years.

In elementary school, Woz was a popular kid with a group of neighborhood friends. They did all the usual kid things: riding their bikes all over town, playing sports, and getting into a bit of mischief.

Woz, in stark contrast to the stereotype of a "young computer whiz," was actually a first-class athlete, following in the footsteps of his football star father.

Woz and his friends loved to ride their bikes
and play games like kickball

But starting in sixth grade, things took a dramatic turn—not for Woz the electronics geek, but for Woz the person.

Up to now, he'd been cruising happily through life. He was the smartest kid in the neighborhood, the smartest in his class, and the other kids respected that. He was good at games and sports, and that gained him respect, too. But in the sixth grade, something changed. It wasn't him, Woz thought, it was everybody else.

The guys started talking about girls. And getting together with the other kids was turning into something else. It wasn't play anymore, it was something he didn't understand—it was socializing.

Woz didn't get it. He had always been a little shy, but now it was like his shyness was multiplied by ten. His technical accomplishments, once something everyone could relate to and admire, stopped mattering much to his peers. He felt invisible.

It continued into high school. Woz was just bad at socializing and he didn't seem to be able to acquire this mysterious skill. He didn't know how to flirt. He didn't get small talk. He felt increasingly alone and isolated, and he felt powerless to do anything about it. While the other kids were hanging out, partying and drinking, Woz was still doing his electronics thing.

It had always been his passion, but now it became his refuge during some painful years.

Things had always come easily to Woz, but overnight things had become very hard, at least when it came to the part of life that's about people, not machines.

Woz was always a problem solver. Although his discomfort with socializing and small talk would never completely go away, he did find a few ways to cope. As always, there were the science projects to keep him going.

And he made another discovery. He realized that he could relate to people by making jokes. Those jokes were critical to his having social relationships at all, so he turned the joking up a notch. "I made people laugh by pulling pranks on them," said Woz. That was his way of trying to connect. He *invented* elaborate pranks the way he invented electronic gadgets. Some of them *were* electronic gadgets.

He pulled pranks throughout middle school and high school. Once he built a device that generated the noise of a police siren and installed it so that it would sound during driver's education while students were using driving simulators.

That prank couldn't have caused much trouble, even if the teachers may not view the memory as fondly as Woz does.

In his senior year, one of Woz's projects was an electronic metronome. It occurred to him that its ticking sounded like the ticking of a bomb. To Woz, this suggested possibilities.

So he attached a couple of batteries, removed their existing labels and relabeled them "CONTACT EXPLOSIVE."

Then, of course, he hid it inside a school locker, not his own, and left it happily ticking away to terrify anyone who came near. Oh, and he added a switched resistor that would speed up the ticking if the locker door was opened. Just for a little added excitement.

Later that day, he was called into the principal's office. In a moment that is uniquely Woz, he remembers being uncertain if the visit was related to the prank's discovery or if it was to tell him he'd won a math contest he'd entered.

When a police officer walked in carrying Woz's device, Woz got the picture. An English teacher had heard the ticking. The principal had opened the locker and, with the "bomb" clutched to his chest, had bravely run outside the building and dismantled the contraption out on the football field. He discovered that it was a prank, and was not amused.

How did they know it was Woz?

At first, they didn't. They suspected another student who was involved in electronics. They called him out of class, showed him the device and accused him of being the perpetrator. He denied it, and he added that the electrical circuits involved looked like Woz's work.

Though he was always a prankster and class clown, Woz graduated high school with excellent grades

It looks like Woz's work. It was something that people would say, as high praise, years later about computer designs. Woz's work was electronic artistry. Even in high school, his electronic designs were uniquely recognizable.

Woz spent that night in juvenile detention. Had he pulled that same prank today, the consequences would no doubt have been much worse. Even in those more innocent days before terrorist threats became such a common worry, he was punished, but he wasn't suspended or expelled.

Of course, Woz made use of his time in juvie. He made friends in this new way that he'd invented: pranks. He showed the other kids how they could rewire a ceiling fan so that it delivered a shock to any officer who touched the bars of a cell.

This experience didn't dampen Woz's enthusiasm for pranks. He wasn't scared straight by punishment, and he certainly didn't mend his ways. Pranks were his new way of fitting in and showing off. As we'll see, he kept pranking people despite the risk of being caught. And his prank-creating technical skills worked for him as a roundabout, if misguided, way to connect with people.

The pranks may also have helped him deal with another problem. He couldn't do what he really wanted to do: build a computer. All of his pranks involved cheap, readily available parts. Computers, on the other hand, the machines he really, really wanted to build, required parts that were priced beyond what he could afford.

Amazingly enough, the fact that he couldn't get those expensive parts didn't bring Woz's obsession with computer design to a dead halt. He could still *design* sophisticated machines on paper, and he took to that activity with a vengeance. Beginning in high school, he stayed up nights, turning out version after version of computer circuitry, making each version simpler, more economical and more efficient than the one before, collecting all the computer manuals he could get his hands on so that he could refine the technology design that was out there already.

Woz would sit and read computer manuals
to give him ideas for his paper designs

While still a teenager, Woz was designing fully-functional computers that were just as powerful as—and more efficient than—the hundred thousand dollar machines the size of a refrigerator created by teams of professional electrical engineers.

Woz kept at it for months and months. He grew more and more confident in his ability to come up with design tricks that professionals could not, with the same parts.

He redesigned existing, commercial computers using half the chips of the original versions. He was showing up professional engineers.

For those who could understand them, these were designs that you could love. They were not just skillful but actually artful in their efficiency. If you wanted to save money, you could build your machine with the absolute minimum of very expensive chips. If you wanted to add power and had money to burn, Woz's designs left room for additional chips in the same small package. Woz was becoming a highly-skilled and experienced computer designer.

Of course this was all just on paper. He had never built a single computer. But that was about to change.

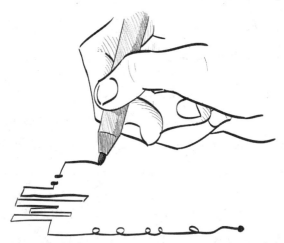

Woz spent hours drawing out circuits on paper in the hope that he'd one day be able to build them

Chapter 4
Soda and Steves

Calling Woz's circuits-on-paper a hobby doesn't do it justice. It was a consuming activity. It was an obsession that took great dedication, and it lasted for a couple of years past high school.

Woz had, in the meanwhile, made a couple of stabs at college and kept doing his paper designs throughout, but the idea was never to settle for the best possible designs without putting those designs to work. The problem always came down to the difficulty and expense of getting the chips he needed.

Two years after graduating from high school, Woz, then out of school, found himself a job as a programmer with a company called Tenet. He'd been impressed by a display of a refrigerator-sized computer at their offices.

Somehow, perhaps because the details of everyday life got less of Woz's attention than the details of a circuit board, he thought he was applying for work at a different and much bigger company, Data General. The misidentification was but a blip on the radar in the end. Tenet fit the bill, and at least they agreed to hire him.

While at Tenet, he made no secret of the paper designs he was doing in his spare time. While he kept up the hunt for actual chips, no company was willing to just hand them out to random hobbyists who approached out of the blue.

Finally, though, Woz did the thing that now seems like an obvious move. He asked one of Tenet's executives, and his wish was granted, presumably out of a supply of samples the executive had on hand.

Woz didn't want to be greedy, though, or abuse the executive's good will, so he set his sights on building a computer with very few chips.

Thus was born the "Cream Soda Computer," so called because Woz and a friend would head out from the garage where they were working and buy lots of Cragmont cream soda—he still remembers the brand—to keep them going while they assembled the device.

Woz and his friend named their computer after the cream soda they drank while building it

By today's standards, the Cream Soda computer wasn't much of a machine. It was a little circuit board, with circuits designed by Woz, of course, and just a few inches square. At the time, a normal computer would have hundreds of chips. This one had only a handful. Among those chips was something amazingly advanced for its time, random-access memory (RAM.) Memory technology back then was generally magnetic core, a technology that relied on finicky voltage adjustments to do its job. Woz wanted no part of that kind of inelegant computing.

Back then, RAM was something special, and Woz had a lot of it, a whole 256 bytes worth. It's fair to say that he felt like he was rolling in RAM, and for those days, he was. To give you an idea of how much things have changed, storing the sentence you're reading right now would take up almost the entire amount of memory the Cream Soda Computer had on board.

The Cream Soda Computer doesn't look like much to us today, but it was a computer. It could run simple programs, like a program that told it to beep every three seconds. It had no screen and no keyboard, like today's personal computers have, and even in its utter simplicity and questionable usefulness, it was a success to Woz.

The device wasn't necessarily useful, but it worked, and it worked as a computer. That was the bottom line. Woz had done what he'd set out to do, and he was ready to tackle the next project.

Woz's friend Bill Fernandez helped him build his first computer

But the Cream Soda Computer was important for one big reason beyond its place in Woz's computer-building story. It was the machine that brought about the fateful meeting between the two Steves, Wozniak and Jobs.

Bill Fernandez, the neighborhood friend who'd helped Woz with his build, suggested that the two Steves meet. Jobs lived about a mile away. He was still in high school at the time, four years behind Woz, but Bill thought they'd get along because they had so much in common. Both Steves enjoyed building electronics. Both liked pranks.

So, on a sunny California day, the two Steves were sitting on the sidewalk in front of Bill's house, sharing stories of pranks and designs.

Woz first met Steve Jobs outside his friend's house because they both loved pranks and computers

Woz could not have been happier. He'd always been frustrated by the fact that kids his age didn't understand what he was talking about when he described his designs. Jobs, however, got it immediately. Imagine what a relief this must have been for Woz, the kid who'd fallen from popularity to invisibility a few years earlier and still felt terribly shy in many social situations.

After a good long time in conversation, Woz brought his new friend into the garage to show him the computer he'd built. Jobs loved what he saw, and both Steves were utterly captivated by the idea that this little circuit board could be an actual computer.

You didn't need a machine as big as a refrigerator. Here was proof that a computer could be a device small enough to put on your desk—maybe not right now, but someday soon, for sure.

Anyone passing those two kindred spirits sitting there on the sidewalk wouldn't have given them a second thought. To a random passerby, they were just two kids talking about girls or sports or whatever it was that kids talked about. There seemed to be nothing momentous going on.

And maybe one of the two Steves had an inkling that the two of them could do something together that one of them couldn't do alone, and that, just maybe, this could be the start of something big.

Chapter 5
The College Try

That sidewalk meeting was important, but it didn't bear fruit immediately. The decision to found a computer giant and name it after a fruit was still years away.

Steve Jobs was still in high school. Woz had already been out for a couple of years. In the midst of working and doing all the projects that meant so much to him, he was still trying to get his formal education under control.

He took his first stab at college at the University of Colorado at Boulder, getting there in a way that looks nothing like the systematic approach you'd expect from a budding engineer. Instead, ending up at Boulder came almost by accident, and it had more to do with weather than with anything about the school itself.

At Woz's high school, seating arrangements were alphabetical, so students always sat near the same group of people. Woz made friends with some of the kids that sat near him. Their names were all near the end of the alphabet and they planned to tour some California schools. One of them suggested something different: the college his father had gone to. Why not check out Colorado?

With only that shaky rationale behind them, they made the trip. They flew to Denver, took a taxi to Boulder, and arrived well after dark. Woz had never been out of California before, but he couldn't see much of what surrounded him that night.

In the morning, though, he experienced another dramatic first. It had snowed some eighteen inches overnight. Woz had seen a few snowflakes before, but nothing like this, and he was captivated. The campus looked beautiful. He loved walking around in the snow, and he loved having a snowball fight that morning. Then and there, Woz made his decision, and all because of snow.

After a snowstorm, Woz fell in love with Colorado and decided he wanted to go to college there

But Colorado was a problem. It was enormously expensive for an out-of-state student, and his dad wasn't sold on Woz's plan.

Woz and his parents compromised. Woz could spend a year in Boulder, but then he'd come back to California and spend his sophomore year at De Anza Community College.

So Woz was off to Colorado, ready to take advantage of all the university had to offer. He lived in a dorm, went to class, made friends, and even went to football games, but it wasn't long before he heard the irresistible lure of the prank calling again.

This time, the prank evolved from a little device that a friend's father had designed over the previous summer. It was a circuit including a couple of resistors, a transistor, a capacitor, and a coil that emitted a signal in the TV frequency range. Using that design, Woz built a couple of devices that could be tuned. Turn a dial to the right frequency, and you could interrupt the signal of a TV that was using that frequency on a particular channel.

Ultimately, he miniaturized the device so that it was no bigger than a 9-volt battery, and the only hint that it wasn't a battery was an external wire that served as an antenna.

Woz dubbed the device the "TV Jammer," because that's exactly what it did. He tried it out on a friend's TV, and he was able to use the jammer to turn the screen black.

That was just a pre-launch test, though. It was hardly a prank if you weren't fooling people, so Woz ventured into a dorm with a big color TV in a common room. When Woz, sitting in the dark at the back of the room, turned the jammer on, it didn't blacken the picture completely. It did "fuzz it up" significantly.

As Woz continued messing with the TV over the next few months, a pattern developed. He'd interfere with the picture and people would do all sorts of things to try to fix it. All the while, Woz would turn the jammer on and off in tandem with people's actions. If someone wacked the side of the TV, Woz might stop the

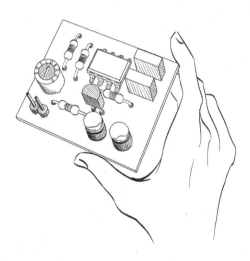

Woz worked to shrink his TV Jammer down
from index card-sized to battery-sized

jammer and let the TV return to normal, leaving the mistaken impression that the right whack would do the trick. If a couple of people tried standing in different spots and the TV suddenly worked, it wasn't their positions that mattered, it was Woz, but he could keep them doing all sorts of comically useless things for as long as he wanted to keep playing the puppeteer.

Two incidents may have soured Woz a little on the TV Jammer experience, though.

The first happened when he jammed that big color TV in the middle of the home stretch of the Kentucky Derby, a prank that led to a near riot, complete with chair throwing, that led Woz to fear for his safety had he been discovered.

The second happened when he used the jammer during one of his computer classes. To his astonishment, the teaching assistant running the class realized what was happening immediately. By that time, Woz had reduced the size of the device to the size of a marker, so he was able to avoid discovery, but it was a close call that might have had unpleasant repercussions.

That wasn't Woz's only trouble with computers in academia. His other misstep had a more serious consequence. Woz had written some programs that did massive amounts of calculations, outputting ridiculously long series of numbers.

Woz was almost kicked out of college for running a program too long at the University of Colorado's computer center

At the school's Computer Center, programs that took more than sixty-four seconds to run were automatically terminated, so Woz designed his programs to run for sixty seconds, print the first sixty pages of numbers and run again, taking another sixty seconds, printing another sixty pages, and so on until the program had finished.

After he'd accumulated reams of computer printouts, he arrived at the Computer Center to be greeted by a message that his professor needed to see him right away! To Woz, what he'd been doing was exactly what any budding engineer would do. He was using computers in the way they were meant to be used. It was all part of programming, and he was taking a programming class. What could be more natural?

To his professor, what Woz had done amounted to theft. It turned out that computer time was strictly allocated and that Woz had run his class's budget five times over its allocation. The professor's solution was that his parents should be billed for the excess time, a bill in the thousands of dollars that was many times bigger than Woz's out-of-state tuition.

Woz didn't want that bill to appear on his parents' doorstep, and that was enough to convince him to forego another year at Colorado. Even today, Woz looks back on using the school's computers to run programs he created as a reason for praise, not blame, and he has a vivid memory of the A+ he received in his programming class.

Woz and college made for an uneasy match. There was never any question about the academic side of things. He was certainly smart enough. He worked hard, even passionately, at the courses he took. The rough patches came from the other side of life, the side in which he interacted with the flawed, often illogical world of flesh and blood.

Perhaps Woz needed time to grow up a little, but none of that was going to stop him from diving head-first into the digital world in which he felt so at home.

Chapter 6
<u>Narrow Escape</u>

Maybe this sounds like it's one of those stories about the young genius who's so precocious that he drops out of school before he's barely moved into his dorm room. Maybe it seems like a story about the prodigy who goes on to fame and fortune despite his lack of formal education. Actually, the story of Woz is not quite that story.

He went back to school at local De Anza College for his second year, then at University of California, Berkeley, for his third year. He loved his classes, looking back on his junior year as his best school year ever. What made it so great, though, wasn't just the academic side of college.

Woz also made friends, and his popularity was largely the result of his adventures in something called "phone phreaking."

To understand phone phreaking, you have to travel back in time to an age before cell phones, the Internet, and any number of technologies we take for granted today. In the days of Woz's youth, communications options were limited.

There was mail, the kind of mail that consists of pieces of paper delivered by the postman to your home or office. There were telegrams, largely reserved for emergencies and for communicating congratulations or condolences, and there was, of course, the telephone.

Woz liked figuring out how to trick the phone company

All telephones were wired, and the network that connected them was the network of a monopoly run by Bell Telephone, "Ma Bell," as it came to be called. Today, you might have a calling plan that allows you to make unlimited calls to anywhere in the world. Back then, calls beyond your area code cost extra.

Some calls even required the assistance of operators, actual humans who sat at switchboards and made the connections for you. Calls to faraway places were called "long distance," and each extra minute of connection cost extra money. Rates changed depending on the time of day you called. The minutes could add up rather quickly.

As a result, people had all kinds of tricks and strategies to help them avoid extravagant phone bills. They'd postpone their calls until late at night, for example, regardless of any inconvenience.

One of those tricks, though, ruled them all. With the right technology, you could make phone calls to any place at any time for free. What you needed was a box that mimicked the tones that the phone company used to give phones—and the network that connected them—their instructions. In effect, having one of these boxes, either the blue box for outgoing calls or the black box for incoming, gave you access to the network without the intrusion of the phone company's vast apparatus for tracking and billing.

This was right up Steve Wozniak's alley. After all, years before this he'd been the one to rig up an entire communications network, primitive though it was, among all the neighborhood kids. He dug into the technology behind the blue box, and, soon enough, he was building them himself.

Woz and his friends used a tool called
a blue box to make phone calls for free

Steve found that he could sell the boxes at a tidy profit, so he went into business with an old buddy, the same buddy whose name pops up frequently in Woz's life, none other than Steve Jobs. The two of them sold the boxes to Woz's fellow Berkeley students, acting something like door-to-door salesmen and going from dorm room to dorm room. Woz made friends throughout the phone-phreaking community.

Interestingly enough, especially in light of their later roles in corporate life, Woz was the one who gave the sales presentations to their prospective customers. Jobs took a back seat. Later, of course, Jobs was the marketing wizard and the face of Apple. It was the most complete and dramatic role reversal imaginable.

Whatever their roles, what Woz and Jobs were doing was utterly illegal. Perhaps it didn't feel like outright theft. At least it never felt personal. After all, the victim was the monolithic phone company, one of the biggest organizations on the planet, a monopoly that was soon to be broken up by the government.

While Woz couldn't deny the criminal side of the enterprise, he didn't see that side as the important thing about it. "I didn't want to steal from the phone company," he said some years later. "I wanted to . . . use their system to exploit flaws in the system."

Woz and Jobs sold boxes to other students at Berkeley, and soon they were all over campus

Had he been caught, that rationale wouldn't have helped him at all, but it was a Woz-like attitude. He loved tech. He loved mischief, especially when it angered the powers-that-be. Phone phreaking was an almost irresistible temptation and, in the end, he and his partner in crime managed to avoid the authorities throughout their phone-phreaking venture.

That doesn't mean that there weren't close calls, and one close call had far-reaching repercussions.

One night, the two partners were returning home in Jobs's car from a trip down south when the car broke down. They found a phone booth and, being phone phreaks, they used the box they had with them to call a friend for help. Instead of reaching that friend, they had trouble with the call. It wouldn't connect; there were strange noises on the line, and suddenly the police were there, asking them to get out of the car.

Jobs handed the box to Woz, who stuffed it into a pocket, but the police found it anyway when they decided to search the two men. They would have been arrested, but they managed to convince the officers that the box was a music synthesizer. Nothing illegal there, right?

Amazed at their ability to pull off the deception, and after some hours with the cops, they were back on the road and made it back to Jobs's house, where Woz had left his own car.

Woz was awfully tired at this point. Driving home in his Ford Pinto, he fell asleep and crashed. While Woz was unscathed, the crash totaled the car.

Woz needed that car. He said that the crash motivated him to go back to work instead of returning to school. He felt a need to make money both to pay for college and buy a new car. If not for the crash, "I wouldn't have quit school, and I might never have started Apple," he said.

So go to work he did, starting at a small electronics company. He wouldn't stay there long, as he was soon offered a chance to work for his dream company.

Strangely enough, that dream job would take him farther away from computers than he'd ever been before, and it took some doing to get him back on the track that ultimately led to fame and fortune.

HP was also a company that started in a garage in the area that would become Silicon Valley

Chapter 7
Do It Yourself Dreams

Allen Baum, Woz's old friend from the neighborhood, was still looking out for him. Allen had helped Woz with a lot of pranks and now he was working at Hewlett-Packard, the coolest electronics company in the Valley, and he helped Woz get a job there.

Woz was finally an engineer, just like his dad, and he was working at Hewlett-Packard! HP, as everybody called it, was an engineer's company. It had been started by a couple of engineers, it made products for engineers, and everybody he worked with was an engineer, like Woz.

Well, not just like him. Not really. Woz was one year away from finishing his college degree, so he wasn't a real engineer yet. Also, since he wasn't a real engineer, the pay was pretty low. He wasn't designing computers, which had been his real love since he was a kid. Still, he felt lucky to be doing engineering work at such a great company.

Of course he was still the Woz, and he still loved jokes and pranks. One of his pranks went on for two years. That was his dial-a-joke phone service.

He rented an answering machine and recorded a new joke every day. Then he told a few friends to try calling the phone number he assigned to the service. Before long, two thousand people

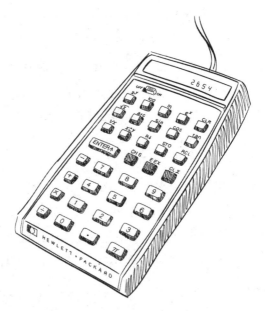

HP mostly created engineering and graphing calculators
when Woz worked there, which were very expensive

a day were calling in to hear that day's joke. Sometimes he picked up the phone and answered the call himself, telling a joke and then engaging the caller in conversation. He was having a ball.

Work was fun, too, but as much as he loved his job, in the three years he'd been at HP, he'd almost forgotten how much he loved computers. How his childhood bedroom had been plastered with pictures of his favorite computers. How he spent hours designing computers on paper. And the Cream Soda computer! He'd actually designed and built a real computer, and it actually worked.

At HP, he was working on calculators. Personal computers were just a dream—no ordinary person owned a computer. But hand-held calculators were crazy popular at the time. In the past couple of years, the price had dropped from hundreds of dollars to tens of dollars. Of course, those cheap ones just did simple math. HP calculators of the kind Woz worked on were designed for engineers and scientists and could do advanced math, even simple programming.

There was a chip inside that was like the brain of a little computer. They weren't computers, but they were pretty cool technology. And Woz got to work on them!

Woz was doing engineering in his spare time, too. For example, he designed a computer terminal. That was how you interacted with a computer then: you used a terminal. It was basically a screen and keyboard combination that could talk to a computer—if you could get access to a computer. Like everything he designed, Woz's terminal was elegant and clever. But it wasn't a computer.

One day, Allen told him about a new club forming for people interested in computer terminals. It was meeting in some guy's garage up the peninsula in Menlo Park. Woz decided to go.

It wasn't what he expected. These people were mostly older than him, experienced engineers who seemed to know about things he knew nothing about. His shyness came out. He didn't say much.

Chris Espinoza was one of Woz's Homebrew friends
and encouraged him in his designs

Woz was more comfortable hanging out with younger people like Chris Espinosa and Randy Wigginton, two kids still in high school who shared his love of computers and programming.

Also, nobody was talking about computer terminals. All they seemed to want to talk about was something called the Altair computer built by a company called MITS. Somebody waved around the latest issue of

Popular Electronics magazine with a picture of this Altair computer on the cover.

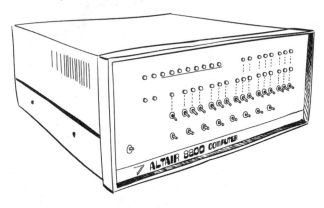

MITS released the Altair computer in 1974, which made Woz realize that he could sell his designs too

It turned out that some company in Arizona was selling a computer in kit form for a ridiculously low price—just a few hundred dollars. Woz was puzzled. He knew that the parts would cost more than that. He got his hands on the magazine and also got a write-up of the processor chip in this Altair computer and took them home to study. When he got done reading the descriptions, he was blown away.

The Altair was no more complicated than his Cream Soda computer! It was simpler, in a way, because the Cream Soda computer used several chips as its brain, the Altair used just one, a new microprocessor called the 8008. Woz realized that he could do what these MITS people did. He could build something better than this Altair. He knew he could.

But there was a problem. Money. The processor alone cost hundreds of dollars, and that was just the start. He wasn't living at home any more, where his dad could help support an expensive hobby. He was supporting himself, and, without a college degree, he was not earning much at HP. He would have to get creative to make this work. So that's what he'd do. He began to design his next computer.

The Homebrew Club was meeting every two weeks now, and hundreds of people were attending. It had to move from the garage to a lecture hall at the Stanford Linear Accelerator Center. Woz went to every meeting. It became the biggest thing in his life. Still shy, Woz always sat near the back row. He took along his friends Chris and Randy—he was their ride, since they were too young to drive.

The Homebrew Club met to discuss computers,
terminals, and programming

Other people at the meetings were working on projects, too. People were writing computer software, they were designing storage and memory products to work with the Altair, they were designing computers to compete with it, and they were starting companies.

An older engineer named Lee Felsenstein—he was at least thirty—ran the meetings, almost like a ringmaster. There was always a lot of lively discussion. And one of the topics of discussion was always where to get parts.

At one meeting, Woz heard about an upcoming electronics conference in San Francisco. Supposedly an engineer named Chuck Peddle was going to sell a microprocessor called the 6502 at the conference for the unheard-of price of $25. Woz had to see this for himself, so he attended the show. He found Chuck and his wife in a nearby hotel room, sitting at a table with two glass jars full of the microprocessors. Woz handed them $25 and went home with the brain for his computer.

In order to make the computer do anything, it would need software. He needed a language that would accept simple commands and convert them into instructions the 6502 could understand.

There wasn't one. For the Altair, some guy named Bill Gates had written a version of the Basic programming language that could talk to the 8008 processor. So Woz wrote from scratch a version of the Basic programming language just for the 6502. And he threw in some features Gates's Basic didn't have.

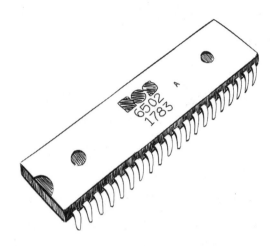

The 6502 microprocessor was the brain chip
of the first Apple computer

Meanwhile, he was working at HP and designing his computer, and he, Chris, and Randy were going to Homebrew meetings every two weeks. He spent hours getting every detail of the design perfect. Sometimes he would completely redesign it because one wire crossed over another in a way that was ugly to his eyes. He was creating something beautiful.

Using Woz's Basic, Chris wrote demo programs to make the computer do things. At every Homebrew meeting, they showed what they had done, and showed what Woz's computer could do.

The Homebrewers were impressed. Woz was happy. He'd built a computer! And people liked it! In fact, they wanted it. To Woz, that was easy. These guys were engineers and computer hobbyists. His design was, as usual, very detailed and clear. All he needed to do was give them his design and they could build their own. And that's what he did.

Steve Jobs had been attending the Homebrew meetings, too. He saw all these people starting companies and he saw an opportunity. He told Woz he shouldn't give away his creation. They should build computers and sell them.

Woz didn't care about the money. He just knew he had done something admirable. Something people appreciated. He wasn't feeling so shy now.

Chapter 8
Apple

Woz and Jobs were going nuts building computers for Homebrew club members in their spare time. Really, they were just hand-wiring the circuit board that was the important part of the computer Woz had designed. But it still took forever. When you added the time spent on their day jobs, they were putting in sixty hours per week.

Jobs had a bright idea. Rather than hook up all the wires by hand, they could pay someone to print circuit boards for them. It was how serious electronics companies did it. A machine, working from a design, actually printed copper tracks on plastic. The copper tracks took the place of the wires, so the board was already wired and all you had to do was solder a few chips in place. Getting printed circuit boards would save them a ton of time, and they could buy the boards for $20 and sell them for $40.

The trouble was the setup process. Woz knew that getting the design into the machine and getting it ready to start printing up boards would cost them about $1000. They didn't have $1000, and even if they did, could they hope to earn that back by selling $40 boards to Homebrewers? It didn't seem likely.

But Jobs was good at talking people into things, and he convinced Woz. Jobs sold his old Volkswagen van and Woz sold his two HP calculators to raise money. Those HP scientific calculators were expensive back then, selling for hundreds of dollars. They paid for the PC board setup and by January were selling finished boards to the Homebrewers.

Woz was proud to have built a functioning, useful computer

If they were going to sell stuff, they figured they should have a real company. They signed papers to form a company on April Fool's Day in 1976. They called it Apple.

But Woz was concerned. If they had a company now, he had to offer his computer to HP. He was an HP employee and his contract required it. He nervously presented the Apple computer to his boss. He had already tried to talk his boss into buying his boards and designs a few times before, but now he had a completed computer to offer. His boss said the Apple computer wasn't right for HP. Woz was free to sell it.

Woz and Jobs created the Apple computer company so that they could sell Woz's designs

That July, Woz did a demonstration of this Apple computer at Homebrew. He was scared, but he was confident, too. He knew his computer was good.

It went well. Of course, many of the people in the group were designing their own computers and starting companies, too. But the Apple computer was impressive.

Jobs was especially interested in one guy in the audience. He went over after the demo and asked the guy what he thought. Jobs even gave him a personal demo of the computer.

Paul Terrell's Byte Shop was the first store to sell Apple computers

The guy, Paul Terrell, owned a computer store down the road. Actually, he owned a bunch of computer stores. Computers were already starting to become a real business, not just a thing for electronics hobbyists.

Terrell had opened his store, the Byte Shop, in December and had already made enough money to open several other stores. A national magazine had published a story about him and these new "personal computers." He was a kind of celebrity.

Jobs nagged him. You should sell our computer, Jobs said. It will be your biggest seller.

Terrell didn't promise anything, but he told Jobs to keep in touch.

The next day, Jobs was in Terrell's office, barefoot. He wasn't into shoes much back then. "I'm keeping in touch," he said.

Terrell liked Job's enthusiasm. And he liked Woz's computer. On the spot, he placed an order for fifty computers. He wanted them delivered, fully assembled, in thirty days. Screen, keyboard, case, the whole works. And he would pay five hundred dollars a computer.

When Jobs told Woz, he was blown away. Their new company already had its first order, and it was for $25,000! That was more than HP was paying Woz per year.

Jobs and Dan Kottke began attending conventions to sell the Apple computers

But only thirty days? And fully assembled? They were back to sixty-hour work weeks.

Plus, Woz had already started designing a new computer, the Apple II. The original Apple had proven that he could design and build a personal computer. The Apple II was going to really show everyone what he could do.

Meanwhile, they had to deliver fifty computers. They were going to need help. They got Allen Baum, Jobs's little sister Patti, and Jobs's friend Dan Kottke from college to help build the computers. They set up an assembly line in Jobs's parents' garage.

Steve Jobs, Woz, and their friends worked hard to build computers in Jobs's parents' garage

And they delivered on time, sort of. Some of the computers they delivered weren't fully assembled. They just didn't have time. But Terrell didn't mind. He could finish the assembly and sell all the Apple computers they had delivered and make a nice profit.

Jobs knew what that meant: there was a real market for personal computers. This was going to be a big business. It wouldn't just be hobbyists buying circuit boards. Computer stores like Terrell's would be selling personal computers to consumers and business users. Jobs wanted Apple to be in the front lines of this revolution.

Woz saw something different. To him, it was about creating something new. His new computer, the Apple II, would have color. And games. And it would be a work of engineering art. It would be a professional design and would be professionally built, like the machines he helped build at HP. It would be the computer he wanted for himself.

But in a funny way, they were both saying the same thing: Let's get serious.

Then suddenly things got very serious. Jobs had been talking to experienced tech business people about their little company. They steered him to a man named Mike Markkula. Markkula was in his thirties but was already a retired millionaire. He had made a lot of money working for Intel, a semiconductor company. He agreed with Jobs that there was a revolution coming. Amazingly, he also agreed that Apple could lead that revolution.

Mike Markkula knew that Apple could revolutionize the personal computer with their designs

In just a few weeks, Markkula had joined Apple as a partner, invested a quarter of a million dollars, and started hiring staff. He told them that they were going to be one of the 500 largest companies in America in five years.

Mike Markkula invested in Apple
and began preparing it to be a huge company

To Woz, it was dizzying. And it got even crazier when Markkula told him he had to quit his job.

This isn't a hobby any more, Markkula said. If we're going to get serious, you have to quit HP. It's HP or Apple. Make your choice.

Woz was devastated. He wanted to design computers. He wanted Apple to succeed. But he loved HP. He had imagined that he would work there all his life. He just couldn't quit. He couldn't.

He told Markkula his decision. If he had to choose between Apple and HP, then he would choose HP.

Chapter 9
Apple Launches and a Crash Landing

Everybody was after Woz to quit his job.

Steve Jobs was determined to keep the Apple team together. He soon convinced all of Woz's friends to help. He had them call Woz and try to talk him into leaving HP. Jobs even got Woz's mom and dad to nag him about it.

But Woz loved HP and intended to work there forever. Having his own company with Steve Jobs and Mike Markkula — sure, that was exciting. But he couldn't see why he had to leave his dream job at HP. If he had to choose, he chose HP.

It was Woz's old friend Allen Baum who finally changed his mind. Allen was the one who got Woz into HP in the first place. He had always been there for Woz. Allen and his dad had lent Woz and Jobs the money they needed for parts to start building those first Apple I computers to deliver to Paul Terrell.

Without Allen's help, there would have been no Apple and no job at HP. And even before all that, when Woz was in college and was curious about computer languages, Allen had sent him copied pages of computer language manuals to study.

Woz listened to Allen seriously. You don't have to be an executive, Allen told him. You can have your own company and still be an engineer. That sounded good to Woz.

In the end, he changed his mind and quit HP, going all in with Apple. But he told Jobs and Markkula that he didn't want to manage anything. He just wanted to be an engineer and design and build computers. They said that was fine.

Woz got right to work, and by August he had finished designing his new computer, the Apple II. He had even built a working model. Mike Markkula told him it was time to show it off. So now here he was on a plane flying across the country to present his new company's new computer at a computer show in New Jersey. Exciting!

The Apple II had eight expansion slots for people to add things, like floppy disk readers, monitors, or extra memory

On the same plane were other Homebrew hobbyists, some of them in suits, all going to the same show, and all acting like business executives, which they were, of course. But a year earlier, they were all hanging out at the Homebrew club, pursuing their electronics hobby. Now they were serious business people. Even crazier, so was he. Well, sort of.

He was still the same Woz. He loved playing games, and he wasn't going to give that up. This was the beginning of the golden age of arcade video games. That summer, kids across America were going to arcades and dropping their quarters in the slots of these refrigerator-sized game machines and playing *Pong* and Sega's *Moto-Cross* and *Breakout*. Woz loved *Breakout* and decided to see if he could recreate it on the Apple II.

This was an outrageous idea. Arcade games required expensive hardware. They were stand-alone machines designed to do one thing really well. No computer could compete with that kind of specialized hardware.

Woz loved games, so he figured out how
to make game software playable on the Apple II

But Woz succeeded. His *Breakout* was just software. No special hardware at all. Woz was amazed that he could mimic one of those expensive game machines in software on a little personal computer. He didn't usually think about sales and the business side of things, but this time he did. Computer games! This could be a huge market, he thought. And it was a market he could understand. He'd spent a ton of money on games.

Still, having his own company wasn't all fun and games. Woz had a big argument with Steve over slots—the places to insert extra circuit boards to control printers and add memory and other abilities to the Apple II. Woz wanted more slots, but Steve wanted to save money. Woz won that one.

And there was no time for silliness like his dial-a-joke service. Although if he had to give that up, at least he got something out of it: he met a girl. Alice Robertson was Woz's first serious girlfriend. He liked that she understood his jokes. In 1976, Woz and Alice got married.

Woz and Alice were married in 1976,
and Steve Jobs was Woz's best man

Meanwhile Mike Markkula was turning Apple into a real company. He hired Mike Scott to run things as President. He hired dozens of other people, including real engineers with degrees like at HP, and he moved the company into its first real offices. Before that, they'd been operating out of Woz's apartment and Jobs's parents' home.

They officially released the Apple II at the West Coast Computer Faire in January of 1977. With its stylish molded plastic case, it looked nothing like the other personal computers, which were mostly square metal boxes. Even here at this serious show, Woz couldn't resist pulling a prank.

With help from Chris and Randy, he made up a snazzy new computer with all kinds of great features. It was a total fiction, but he printed up hundreds of impressive-looking flyers describing it, and snuck them into the show. Jobs was worried by this impressive-looking competitor. It took him a while to figure out that it was a hoax, and years went by before he learned that Woz had been behind it.

Woz and Jobs were having a blast with their new company, and Woz loved that he was allowed to keep designing and programming

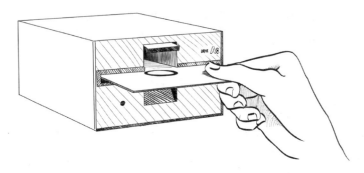

Woz wanted to make a better disk controller than other companies used, so his didn't wait for the disk to speed up

All of 1977, Woz worked on engineering projects, including the floppy disk interface. One big problem personal computers had at this time was storage. Big mainframe computers used expensive disk drives to store programs and data, but most personal computers used something more affordable, like cassette tapes normally used in the tape recorders of the day.

But disk storage was faster and more reliable, and one manufacturer had come out with a small, inexpensive disk drive. If Apple had the software and hardware needed to work with these drives, it would be a big advantage over the competition. It would also make the Apple II a more convincing machine for business users.

Mike Markkula asked Woz to create the disk controller software and hardware.

Woz knew nothing about disk controllers, but he jumped on it. It turned out to be another brilliant and unconventional Woz design.

Disk drives don't run at a constant speed: they speed up when starting up. Woz figured that instead of waiting for the drive to get up to speed he could just read or write the data at whatever speed the disk was going. It meant understanding exactly what was going on with the drive at any millisecond and changing the software to work with it. Nobody did that, but Woz did. He ended up using 1/10 the chips of any other disc controller and made it at a fraction of the cost. With the help of Randy Wigginton, one of his younger friends from Homebrew who began working for Apple, he finished over Christmas 1977, just in time for the Consumer Electronics Show in January.

Apple wasn't just two guys in a garage now. While Woz was finishing the drive, some of the other engineers started work on another computer, and this one wasn't Woz's design. On May 13, 1980, they released the Apple III. It was supposed to be a challenge to IBM, which was rumored to be planning its own personal computer.

IBM was a huge company with tons of money. They would be scary competition, so Apple needed a great business computer. That was the idea behind the Apple III. Unfortunately, it was a disaster. The computer had serious problems. They went back to the drawing board.

Apple was getting ready to get on the stock exchange. That meant there would be stock in the company that would be worth lots of money. As a founder, Woz was entitled to a lot of stock, but many of the friends who had helped out weren't, like Chris and Randy.

Woz came up with a plan to let other Apple employees buy some of his stock for very little money. This was a generous gift to his friends because the stocks were worth a lot, but the money it raised also allowed Woz and Alice to buy a house. Unfortunately, Alice wasn't having fun in the marriage while Woz was spending all his time on Apple. In late 1980, they got a divorce.

Shortly after this, towards the end of 1980, Woz met a young woman named Candi Clark. He was in love again.

Then, in February, something happened that would change his life in an unexpected way. Woz had learned to fly a plane, and he liked to take Candi and his friends for rides. One day while practicing take-offs and landings, something went very wrong. The plane took off and immediately came back down again, hard. Woz, Candi, and another passenger were all injured in the crash. But the seriousness of Woz's injury was greater than anyone knew.

Chapter 10
Back to School in Berkeley

In 1981, Woz was practicing touch-and-go landings with his four-seat single-engine plane at the Scotts Valley airport when he botched a touchdown and crashed the plane. He missed hitting a crowded skating rink by a couple hundred feet. Woz and Candi were injured, but recovered quickly, or so it seemed.

But there was something wrong with Woz. The crash affected his memory. Nobody knew, but for weeks, he didn't even realize he had been in a plane crash. Little by little, he began to get his memory back, but it took weeks.

The time in the hospital and recovering from the accident kept him away from Apple. While he was away, he started to think more about what he was doing with his life. When he went back to work, it wasn't the same.

Apple didn't feel like the friendly place he and Jobs and Mike Markkula had created. In

February of 1981, the same month as the plane crash, company president Mike Scott fired forty people.

Steve Jobs became the face of Apple while Woz was away

Woz liked Scotty and wanted to understand.

The company had grown really fast and maybe they had hired people who weren't really pulling their weight. Maybe Scotty had done the necessary thing in firing those people, but it wasn't done well. It seemed cruel and unfeeling. This way of doing business seemed cruel. Did it have to be?

That summer, Scotty left the company. Mike Markkula had demoted him for his handling of the firings, and he decided Apple wasn't a fun place to be. Woz knew what he meant. He had been unhappy about Scotty firing people, but he didn't want to see Scotty go.

Apple was really turning into a big business. The Apple III was re-released as a business machine to compete directly with IBM's new computer in its own market. No company was more a symbol of men in suits than IBM, and Apple was going into direct competition

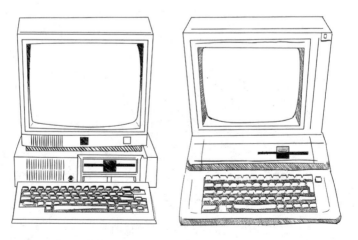

IBM released their new business computer (left) in 1981, but Apple was ready to compete with the Apple III (right)

with them for those business users. The whole industry was changing from a fun hobby into a hard-nosed business. Everyone told Woz that he was worth a hundred million dollars. He couldn't make much sense of that.

Outside Apple, Woz's life was moving ahead. He and Candi got married in June of 1981, and Woz decided to go back to school. In the fall of 1981, he went back to Berkeley to complete his final year of college. He enrolled under the name Rocky Raccoon Clark.

That was actually the name on his registration. It was partly a goof, but partly because he had become a celebrity by now. Apple was big news, and its co-founder would have been a celebrity on campus. He was keeping a low profile.

That year, he and Candi got an apartment near campus, and he became a familiar sight, walking to class with his backpack and Walkman. Few students knew who he was. He got in arguments with teaching assistants who would have been surprised to learn that they were arguing with a computing legend. He was having a great time.

When he finished his degree, he was proud. During those years at HP, he had felt inferior to the engineers with degrees. No, not inferior, but he felt left out. Like the engineers had a club, and

Woz finally graduated college in 1982 with a degree in electrical engineering from University of California, Berkeley

he wasn't in it. He knew he could do things they couldn't, but the degree mattered.

Now, though, when he went back to work at Apple, he felt left out of things again. There was this big push for a new computer called the Macintosh. Woz's computer, the Apple II, was bringing in all the money. It was keeping the company alive. But Jobs was telling everybody that the Macintosh was the future and that anybody working on the Apple II was a loser.

Apple's Macintosh computer introduced
the easy-to-use graphical user interface

Woz talked to the people working on the Macintosh. These young guys looked up to him as a kind of legend. There were some great young programmers and engineers on the team, like Andy Hertzfeld, who was working on the very complicated Macintosh system software. To Andy, Woz was a legend. Woz wasn't sure how that made him feel. It didn't make him feel involved. He felt sidelined and unnecessary.

Steve Jobs was very proud of the Macintosh computers and thought they revolutionized the personal computer

Woz was paying more attention to his home life now. He and Candi moved into a new and bigger house. He began thinking about his other interests. Like music. He wanted to do something with music. He wasn't going to leave Apple officially. He knew he would be loyal to Apple and the people there forever. But he wasn't going in to work. He was checking out.

He needed to find his place in the world apart from Apple.

Chapter 11
Happiness

While he was at Berkeley, Woz decided to put on a music festival.

He had a friend who managed a nightclub in Santa Cruz, and this friend knew a guy who had experience in putting on concerts. Woz gave him two million dollars to get started. It was going to end up costing a lot more.

Woz threw the festival of the year in 1983. Lots of celebrities attended like David Lee Roth from Van Halen

They wanted to create something huge, like the famous Woodstock concert of the 1960s. They found a site near San Bernardino with a big field and a lake, where people could camp for days. They even arranged for a temporary freeway exit just for the concert. There were food vendors, t-shirt vendors, and technology demo tents for tech companies to show off new gadgets. Legendary concert promoter Bill Graham lined up the musicians. Woz called it the US Festival. US, like you and me, not like United States.

In the end, over 400,000 people showed up. Was the US Festival a success? Not financially. Woz lost millions of dollars on it. But everyone had a great time and it was a big influence on future massive concerts like Lollapalooza and Coachella.

Meanwhile, while all the craziness of the concert was going on, Candi had their first child, a baby boy named Jesse, in 1983.

Woz considered the US Festival money well spent. He had more money than he needed, why not spend it to make people happy? He'd shared his wealth with Apple employees early on. Now he started giving money to causes he believed in.

The building of the Children's Discovery Museum
in San Jose was funded primarily by Woz

With Bill Graham, he funded the building of Shoreline Amphitheater, a massive permanent concert venue. He gave millions to help start the Children's Discovery Museum in San Jose. The City of San Jose named a street for him: Woz Way, next to the Museum. He helped start a technology museum and contributed to arts groups in San Jose.

But he wasn't content to just sit back and give money to good causes. Even if he wasn't doing anything at Apple, he still wanted to create

To thank Woz for his donation, the street the
Discovery Museum is on was named Woz Way

things. He got an idea for a universal remote
for controlling anything—a TV, DVD player, or
any device. Just like with the Apple II, he sought
perfection in his work on this remote. New
devices were being invented all the time that you
might want to operate with a remote control. So
he didn't want the buttons on his remote to have
fixed functions. They should be programmable
by the user. He created a tiny language for
programming the buttons. On this device, one
button could even reprogram another button.

He got creative with the hardware, too. He decided the device needed two processors, one 6502 processor like the brain of the Apple II, and one small, cheap 4-bit processor to read the keyboard and do a few other tasks. Programming the little processor was very tricky, but he loved that. The device was not for everybody: it was a nerd's dream.

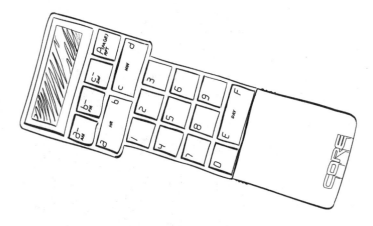

Woz never stopped inventing and programming and actually invented the first programmable remote

To build the device, Woz started a new company, CL9, with just two partners, operating out of a little office above an ice cream store in Los Gatos, not far from where he grew up. It felt like old times. Eventually, when the fun part of designing was done, he sold the company, and went on to help friends out with other startups.

And grown-up life went on. He and Candi had two more kids. Now that he had kids of his own, he wanted to share his love of instruction sets as his father had shared his love of electronics. He turned out to be an inspiring teacher. He had never lost the excitement he had as a kid, and he shared that excitement with his kids.

To share his passion for computers, Woz spent ten years teaching computer classes at local schools

Pretty soon, he was teaching his son Jesse's friends how to use computers. Then he set up computer labs in schools, and then put together an actual class. This multimillionaire computing legend became an elementary school teacher, teaching about binary math and computers.

The ten years he taught in the schools was, he later said, the most important time of his life. But he was still Woz, still the prankster, still dedicated to having fun. Life, he said, is to be enjoyed. He bought a Segway self-balancing scooter when they first came out, and made it a part of his life. People would spot him at computer shows or music events on his Segway. He helped start a whole sport playing polo on Segways, and today the Segway Polo world championship is called the Woz Challenge Cup.

He appeared on the TV show *Dancing with the Stars* and danced the samba.

And he traveled. He was in demand: young programmers and entrepreneurs wanted him to speak to their clubs or classes or companies. And he wanted to see the world. He started thinking about moving to Australia, but the tech excitement of the Bay Area still held him.

Woz didn't make it very far, but he really had fun
dancing on *Dancing with the Stars*

During this period, Apple was going through
some tough times. In the 1980s, Steve Jobs had
a fight with management and went off to start
another company. Then, in the 1990s, Apple
brought Jobs back and seemed to be finding its
way again.

A strange moment came when Woz found
himself standing on a stage with Jobs in front
of thousands of excited fans, the two founders
back with the company. It was a strange magical
moment, but it was just a moment. Woz

wasn't really going back to work at Apple. He'd moved on.

But moved on to what?

He got a chance to explain that when he was invited to give commencement speeches at colleges. He tried to explain what it was all about for him. He wasn't as good a public speaker as Steve Jobs, he didn't even like the idea of giving a speech, but he knew he had something to give people. He had learned some things about life, and he wanted to share them.

When Steve Jobs returned to Apple,
Woz decided he'd rather help people instead

"[Designing computers] was my love in life," Wozniak told Berkeley graduates. "Something you do when you don't get anything for it."

But "a lot of us get successful in life," he said, "We get money, we get wealth, we get fame, like I did. A lot of people become different people than they were."

Woz spoke at Berkeley's graduation ceremony in 2013 and told the young graduates to chase their passion

Not Woz. He offered two formulas for happiness in life:

1) Happiness equals S minus F (smiles minus frowns).

2) Happiness equals F cubed — food, fun and friends.

Childlike, yes. Woz had remained a child at heart. On his website, www.woz.org, he provided a biographical essay. The last line of it reads:

"Loves children and dogs."

Woz and his wife Janet have two dogs, Zelda and Ziggy

Select Quotes from Steve Wozniak

"Some great people are leaders and others are more lucky, in the right place at the right time. I'd put myself in the latter category, But I'd never call myself a normal designer of anything."

—Woz.org, General Questions Answered

"If you love what you do and are willing to do what it takes, it's within your reach. And it'll be worth every minute you spend alone at night, thinking and thinking about what it is you want to design or build. It'll be worth it, I promise."

—*iWoz: Computer Geek to Cult Icon* by Steve Wozniak and Gina Smith

"Soldering things together, putting the chips together, designing them, drawing them on drafting tables—it was so much a passion in my life. And to this day, I'll go stay at the bottom of the organization chart being an engineer, because that's where I want to be."

—*Bloomberg Business* interview, 2014

Steve Wozniak Timeline

1950 August 11   Stephan Gary Wozniak born

1956   First electronics experiment: radio

1959   Won first Science Fair with a home-made flashlight

1960   Tested conductivity using a lightbulb and carbon rods

1961   Won second Science Fair with an interactive table of elements

1962   Built a machine to play tic-tac-toe

1964   Built a machine to add and subtract

1968   Entered college in Colorado

1970   Built his first computer, the Cream Soda Computer

1971   Met Steve Jobs

1972   Built a Blue Box to hack the phone system

1973   Created his Dial-a-Joke service

1975   Attended first Homebrew Computer Club meeting

1976   Built the Apple I computer

1976 January   Married Alice Robertson

1976 April 1   Started a company with Jobs, called it Apple

1980 December   Woz becomes a multimillionaire

1981 February 7   Crashed his private plane, suffered amnesia

1981 June   Married second wife, Candi Clark

1981   Returned to college under an assumed name

World Timeline

1950 June 25   Korean War begins.

1957 October 4   First space satellite, Sputnik, launched.

1957   FORTRAN, the first major computer programming language, is developed

1958   First integrated circuit created.

1960   First laser built by Theodore H. Maiman.

1966 September 8   *Star Trek* debuts.

1967   First handheld calculator developed

1969 July 20   Neil Armstrong walks on the moon.

1969 October 29   First email message sent.

1971 November 15   Intel released first microprocessor

1972 May   Magnavox releases the first home video game console

1972   American, Bobby Fischer, becomes World Chess Champion

1974   Altair computers introduced, starting the age of the personal computer

1977 April 16   Apple II released

1977 May 25   Movie *Star Wars* released

1980 December 12   Apple stock went public

1982   "The Computer" is named Time Magazine's Man of the Year

Steve Wozniak Timeline (cont.)

1982   Put on the first US Festival, a huge music event

1985   Awarded National Medal of Honor by President Reagan

1985   Launched a new company, CL9, to make a universal remote control

1989   Married third wife, Suzanne Mulkern

2000 September   Inducted into the National Inventors Hall of Fame

2003   Invented Segway polo

2008   Married fourth wife, Janet Hill

2009   Contestant on TV show *Dancing with the Stars*

2013   Gave commencement speech at Berkeley

World Timeline (cont.)

1983 June 18   Sally Ride becomes the first American woman in space

1984 January 24   First Macintosh released

1989   Tim Berners-Lee invents the World Wide Web.

1990 April 24   Hubble Space Telescope launched

2001 October 23   iPod released

2001 December   Dean Kamen invented the Segway two-wheeled, self-balancing, battery-powered electric vehicle

2007 June 29   iPhone released

2011 October 5   Steve Jobs died from complications related to pancreatic cancer

Glossary

Apparatus The technical equipment or machinery needed for a particular activity or purpose.

Atoms The basic unit of a chemical element.

Byte A measurement of memory space on a computer.

Capacitor a device used to store an electric charge, consisting of one or more pairs of conductors separated by an insulator.

Carbon rod A rod, made of carbon, used in some types of battery.

Digital logic The representation of signals and sequences of a digital circuit through numbers.

Diode A semiconductor device with two terminals, typically allowing the flow of current in one direction only.

Electron A stable subatomic particle with a charge of negative electricity, found in all atoms and acting as the primary carrier of electricity in solids; a very small particle that moves outside the nucleus of an atom.

Engineer A person trained and skilled in the design, construction, and use of engines or machines.

Enterprise A project or undertaking, typically one that is difficult or requires effort.

Entrepreneur A person who organizes and operates a business or businesses, taking on greater than normal financial risks in order to do so.

Hydroelectric Relating to the generation of electricity using flowing water to drive a turbine that powers a generator.

Magnetic Core Memory   A type of computer memory that uses voltage pulses to store information.

Metronome   A device used by musicians that marks time at a selected rate by giving a regular tick.

Monopoly   Complete control over a service or product within a given area.

Nuclear reactor   Any of several devices that initiate and control a nuclear fission chain reaction to produce energy and material.

Periodic table   A table of the chemical elements so that elements with similar atomic structure appear in vertical columns.

Precocious   Showing qualities or abilities of an adult while still a child.

Prodigy   A person, especially a young one, endowed with exceptional qualities or abilities.

Random Access Memory (RAM)   A type of computer memory that can recall the information in any order.

Resistor   A device designed to introduce resistance into an electric circuit.

Semiconductor   A substance, that is neither a good conductor of electricity nor a good insulator that allows some electricity to flow through it, used in making electronic devices with electrical conductivity.

Solder   Any mixture of metals that is melted and used to connect pieces of metal.

Soldering Iron   A tool used to melt metal to connect pieces of metal.

Transistor   A small device used to control the flow of electric current.

Bibliography

Swaine, Michael, and Paul Freiberger, *Fire in the Valley: The Birth and Death of the Personal Computer*. The Pragmatic Bookshelf, 2014.

Wozniak, Steve, and Gina Smith. *iWoz: Computer Geek to Cult Icon*. W. W. Norton & Company, 2007.

SUGGESTED READING

Blumenthal, Karen, *Steve Jobs: The Man Who Thought Different: A Biography*. Square Fish, 2012.

Shetterly, Margot Lee *Hidden Figures: The American Dream and the Untold Story of the Black Women Who Helped Win the Space Race*. Harper Collins, 2016.

Noyce, Pendred. *Magnificent Minds: 16 Pioneering Women in Science and Medicine*. Tumblehome Learning, Inc., 2016.

Macaulay, David. *The Way Things Work Now*. HMH Books for Young Readers, 2016.

Index

Index (cont.)

Index (cont.)

Index (cont.)

Index (cont.)

Index (cont.)

periodic table of the elements, 11, 12
science fairs, 10
    Adder/Subtractor, 13, 14, 15, 16
    liquid conducting electricity, 10, 11
    periodic table of the elements, 11, 12
Scott, Mike, 80, 87
Segway, 100
selling Apple computers, 68, 69
semiconductors, 72
Silicon Valley, 3
6502 microprocessors, 61, 62
software, 61
    for disk controllers, 83
speeches, 101, 102, 103, 104
Stanford Linear Accelerator Center, 59
starting Apple, 51, 64–74
stock exchange, 84
storage
    disk, 82
    Homebrew Club, 60

T

telephone calls. *See also* phone phreaking
    cost of, 46
    free, 45
    networks, 47
Tenet, 27, 28
terminals, computer, 56, 60
Terrell, Paul, 67, 68, 70, 71, 75
theft
    of computer time, 41, 42, 43
    phone phreaking, 45, 46, 47, 48
timeline, 106–109
transistors, 15, 38
TV Jammer, 38, 39, 40

U

University of California, Berkeley, 44
    graduation from, 90
    re-entry to (1981), 89

Index (cont.)